mighty machines

SPACECRAFT

Written by
Adam Hibbert

Illustrated by
Graham Howells

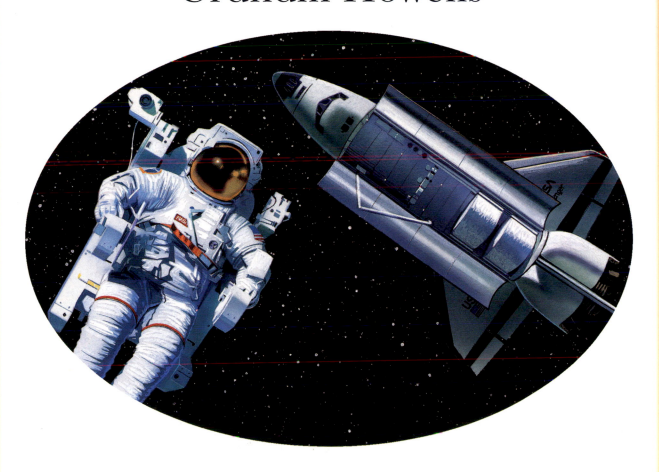

p

This is a Parragon Publishing Book
First published in 2001

Parragon Publishing
Queen Street House
4 Queen Street
Bath BA1 1HE, UK

Copyright © Parragon 2001

Produced by

David West 🏃 Children's Books
7 Princeton Court
55 Felsham Road
Putney
London SW15 1AZ, UK

British Library Cataloguing-in-Publication Data

A catalogue record for this book is available from
the British Library.

ISBN 0-75254-693-7

Printed in U.A.E

Designer
David West
Illustrator
Graham Howells
(SGA)
Cartoonist
Peter Wilks
(SGA)
Editor
James Pickering
Consultant
Steve Parker

CONTENTS

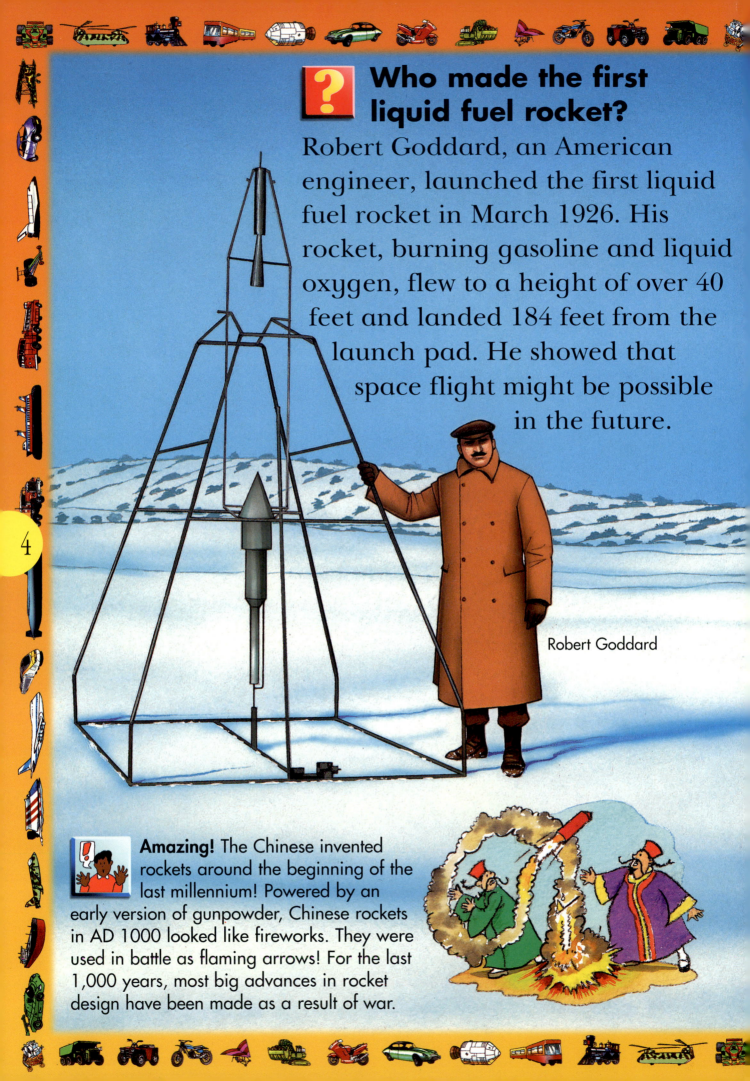

❓ Who made the first liquid fuel rocket?

Robert Goddard, an American engineer, launched the first liquid fuel rocket in March 1926. His rocket, burning gasoline and liquid oxygen, flew to a height of over 40 feet and landed 184 feet from the launch pad. He showed that space flight might be possible in the future.

Robert Goddard

4

Amazing! The Chinese invented rockets around the beginning of the last millennium! Powered by an early version of gunpowder, Chinese rockets in AD 1000 looked like fireworks. They were used in battle as flaming arrows! For the last 1,000 years, most big advances in rocket design have been made as a result of war.

? What did the first satellite do?

Sputnik

Sputnik 1 was launched into orbit by Soviet Russia on October 4th, 1957, 121 days ahead of its American rival, Explorer 1. Sputnik circled the Earth once every 90 minutes, sending radio messages for 21 days, which the world listened to on the radio.

German V2 Rocket

Is it true?
Rockets were used in World War 2.

Yes. The German scientist Wernher von Braun made rockets that could launch bombs across the English Channel. They damaged London without risking the lives of German pilots. Von Braun's V2 rocket was so successful that after the war, America gave him a job helping with its space program.

? Who was the first earthling in space?

Before the first humans went to space, animals paved the way. Laika, a Russian mongrel dog, was the first earthling in space. Her seven days in orbit proved that space travel would be safe for humans.

Laika

❓ What was the biggest rocket ever?

American Saturn 5 rockets were 364-feet tall monsters, weighing 2,903 tons on the launch pad. That's as heavy as 600 elephants! They were more greedy than elephants, too, burning 15 tons of fuel per second. Saturn 5 rockets were used to launch all the Apollo missions to the Moon.

Arianne rocket launching a satellite in space

6

❓ What do rockets carry?

Rocket cargo is called the payload, the load that pays for the trip. Most rockets are designed to carry one or two satellites. Some satellites are for scientific research, some are for communication, and some are for spying. Of course, rockets can also carry people!

Saturn 5

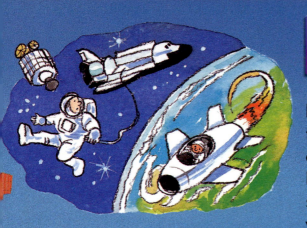

 Is it true?
Jet planes can fly in space.

No. Jet engines need to take oxygen from the air around them to burn fuel. Because there's no air in space, a jet engine wouldn't work up there.

? Why do rockets have stages?

Rockets have to be big to carry enough fuel to escape the Earth's pull. But once the fuel is burnt, those big engines and fuel tanks are useless. Their weight would make visiting the Moon very difficult. So rockets are made in stages, or pieces, which drop off when they've done their job.

Amazing! Three German engineers made a rocket-powered car in 1928! Fritz von Opel, Max Valier and Friedrich Sander tested the first version, Opel-Rak 1, on March 15, 1928. Opel later used the rocket knowledge he learnt from Valier to fit 16 rockets on to a glider plane. It was the second ever rocket-powered aircraft.

Launch escape system

Command module

Service module

Lunar module inside

Stage 3 contains fuel and rocket engines

Stage 2 contains fuel and rocket engines

Stage 1 contains fuel and rocket engines

USA   USA

Saturn 5

❓ Who was the first person in space?

Yuri Gagarin, a 27 year old Soviet pilot, orbited the Earth on April 12, 1961. He spent 90 minutes in space in the Vostok 1 spacecraft before returning safely to Earth. Gagarin ejected from his capsule three miles above ground, landing by parachute near a very surprised six year old girl.

Yuri Gagarin

John Glenn's Mercury capsule

❓ Who was the first American in space?

Alan Shepard just reached space on May 5, 1961. He stayed only a few seconds, but he inspired America to reach for the Moon. John Glenn was the first American to orbit the Earth.

Amazing! You can see the Great Wall of China from space. Especially at sunset and sunrise, the wall casts a very sharp shadow across the Chinese landscape, and is quite visible to the naked eye. Without the help of a telescope, you can also make out city lights, and even supertankers!

Alexei Leonov
leaves his
Voskhod spaceship

? Who made the first space walk?

Alexei Leonov walked in space on March 18th, 1965. He was roped to his space capsule to stop him floating away. His space suit ballooned with air, and he had to let most of it out before he could fit back inside the capsule!

Valentina Tereshkova

Is it true?
Sally Ride was the first woman in space.

No. Valentina Tereshkova, a Soviet Russian textile worker, retrained as a pilot. She blasted into space on June 16th, 1963, staying up in Vostok 6 for nearly three days. Later that year, she married another Soviet space traveller, Andrian Nikolayev. Sally Ride was the first American woman to reach space, on the space shuttle *Challenger*, in 1983.

9

? Who was the first person on the Moon?

Neil Armstrong was the first man to step on to the surface of the Moon, on Sunday July 20th, 1969. Armstrong called it one small step for a man, one giant leap for mankind. He was followed out by Buzz Aldrin, while Michael Collins orbited the Moon above them.

Neil Armstrong

Amazing! There is no wind on the Moon, so flags need a wire along the top to hold them out straight. The first flag was planted by Armstrong and Aldrin. They put it so close to their lander that it was knocked over when they blasted off.

Is it true?
Astronauts played golf on the Moon.

Yes. Apollo 14 arrived on the Moon in February, 1971, flown by Alan Shepard, America's first man in space, and Edgar Mitchell. They took rock samples and did some scientific experiments. After completing all their serious research work, Alan Shepard took out a golf club he had put together, and struck a few balls. They flew 400 yards in the low Moon gravity, much further than they would have done on Earth.

Who took a car to the Moon?

The Apollo 15 crew took a Lunar Rover to the Moon in 1971. David Scott and James Irwin drove the battery-powered car around at speeds up to 7 mph. It had a satellite dish, a TV camera and baskets to carry moon rocks.

Lunar Rover

11

Apollo 13

For whom was the number 13 unlucky?

James Lovell and his crew were flying to the Moon in Apollo 13, on April 13th, 1970, when vital oxygen tanks exploded, disabling the spacecraft. The Moon mission was canceled. Ground Control worked very hard, and managed to bring them home successfully.

❓ How do you fit into a space suit?

Space suits are almost as complicated as spacecraft. They must fit astronauts' bodies well, but they are made about two inches too tall. That's how much longer your spine becomes in weightlessness.

Is it true?
Astronauts get space sickness.

Yes. Weightlessness can confuse your body's senses, making you vomit. Obviously, an astronaut's tummy must settle down before any space-walking is allowed.

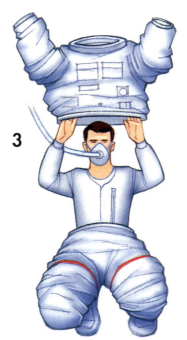

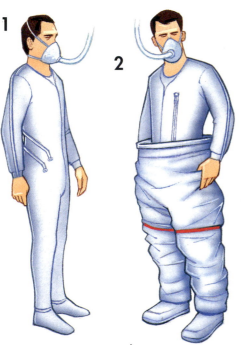

1 Get into special temperature-controlled underwear. **2** Slip on the lower body suit, with space boots, and plug in your diaper. **3** Slip into the top half from below. **4** Lock upper and lower parts together with metal connectors. **5** Put on the radio headset and check the microphone is working. **6** Lock gloves to the suit at the wrist with metal connectors. **7** Add your helmet and lock it into place. **8** Check that life support systems are working before climbing out through an airlock!

Amazing! Since you can't hold your nose in a space suit, it does it for you! There is a device inside the helmet, which pinches your nose if you press against it. Astronauts can use this to hold their noses while they blow, to pop their ears when the pressure changes.

12

? Who trains in a water tank?

Working in a bulky space suit in orbit takes a lot of practice, but there's no room for mistakes in space. So astronauts practice in water tanks on Earth, which gives a feeling of weightlessness.

Underwater training

5

6

7

8

? Why do astronauts need space suits?

Space is a vacuum (it has no air), so it's deadly for humans. Space suits give astronauts air to breathe, keep temperatures comfortable and block radiation. They also stop your body from exploding!

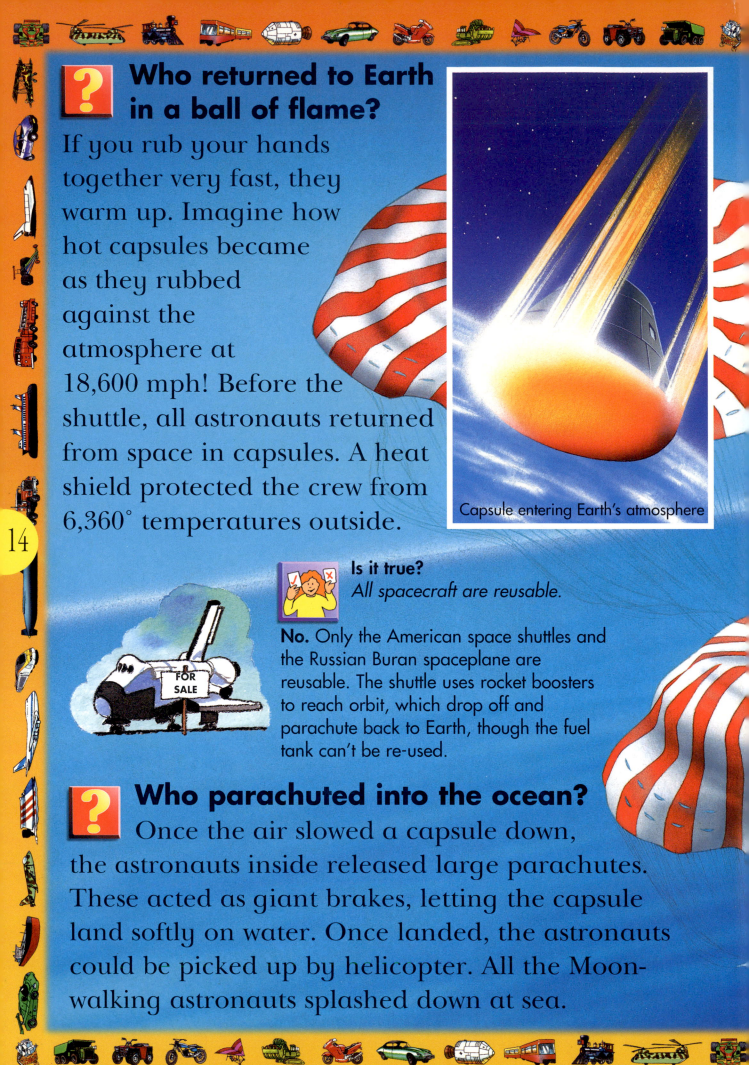

? Who returned to Earth in a ball of flame?

If you rub your hands together very fast, they warm up. Imagine how hot capsules became as they rubbed against the atmosphere at 18,600 mph! Before the shuttle, all astronauts returned from space in capsules. A heat shield protected the crew from 6,360° temperatures outside.

Capsule entering Earth's atmosphere

Is it true?
All spacecraft are reusable.

No. Only the American space shuttles and the Russian Buran spaceplane are reusable. The shuttle uses rocket boosters to reach orbit, which drop off and parachute back to Earth, though the fuel tank can't be re-used.

FOR SALE

? Who parachuted into the ocean?

Once the air slowed a capsule down, the astronauts inside released large parachutes. These acted as giant brakes, letting the capsule land softly on water. Once landed, the astronauts could be picked up by helicopter. All the Moon-walking astronauts splashed down at sea.

? Which space travelers had ejector seats?

Soviet Russia had no safe ocean to use, so cosmonauts had to land on solid ground. They used ejector seats to abandon their plummeting capsule about three miles above ground. Then they parachuted gently to Earth.

Amazing! Russia calls its space travelers cosmonauts, meaning "sailors of the universe". Americans think astronaut is a better word, meaning "sailor of the stars".

What do astronauts eat?

Astronauts take dehydrated (waterless) food into space, which weighs less than normal food. As their spacecraft burns hydrogen and oxygen in orbit, it creates water, which they add to their food. Astronauts eat slowly to stop food flying around!

Mealtime in space

Astronauts testing space station shower

Is it true?

Astronauts can't wash in space.

No. The American Skylab space station (1973-4) had a shower, and so will space stations of the future. Astronauts climbed into a bag to wash, and water was vacuumed away. There are no showers on shuttles though. The crew use wet wipes.

Amazing! Shrimps, spiders, flies, bees, jellyfish, frogs and goldfish have been to space! Animals were first used to test whether space travel would kill humans. The first creature to orbit the Moon was a tortoise!

How long can you stay in space?

Nobody knows! Weightlessness makes your heart lazier and your bones weaker. The biggest danger is radiation, but with exercise and shielding, you could stay in space for ages!

Shuttle docking with Mir space station

How do you go to the toilet in space?

Very carefully! Once you're strapped to the toilet, it draws air into the bowl like a vacuum cleaner. Liquids are shot into space. Solids are taken home.

Which spacecraft is reusable?

The space shuttle was the world's first reusable spacecraft. Instead of a stack of rocket stages, it has separate booster rockets and a big fuel tank. The shuttle drops these before reaching orbit. It eventually glides back to Earth using its wings.

3

3 Eventually the shuttle returns to Earth to be used again.

2

2 The fuel tank is jettisoned and burns up in the atmosphere. This is the only part that isn't reused.

1

1 The rocket boosters detach themselves and float back to Earth by parachute to be reused.

MMU in action

What is an MMU?

The Manned Manoeuvring Unit, or MMU, is a small strap-on spacecraft. Together with a space suit, the MMU lets an astronaut move freely through space. It uses 24 tiny jets of gas to travel in any direction.

Amazing! The shuttle has a special area for cargo. It can hold up to 29 tons. That's the size and weight of an adult humpback whale!

What does the space shuttle do?

The shuttle was first used for taking large satellites into orbit. After one shuttle blew up in 1986, NASA decided to use unmanned rockets again for launching satellites. The shuttle is now devoted to research, repairing satellites in orbit, and to building a space station.

Shuttle nose tiles

Is it true?
The shuttle is protected by tiles.

Yes. The shuttle is made from aluminum. This metal is very light, but it melts at high temperatures. A shuttle can heat up to 6,360° as it returns to Earth, so it needs 20,000 heat proof tiles, which are glued on to its nose and belly.

? What is a satellite?

Anything in orbit around the world is a satellite. Man-made satellites are normally smaller than a car. People make satellites for special jobs. Some study the Earth, some bounce electronic messages around the world, and some are telescopes for studying the universe. Earth has a natural satellite, too – the Moon.

Communications satellite

? How do satellites stay up?

Once satellites have been launched by rocket, they try to zoom off into space, while the Earth tries to pull them down. The two movements added together balance out, making the satellite travel in a circle, called the orbital path.

Pull of Earth's gravity stops satellite flying off

Orbital path of satellite

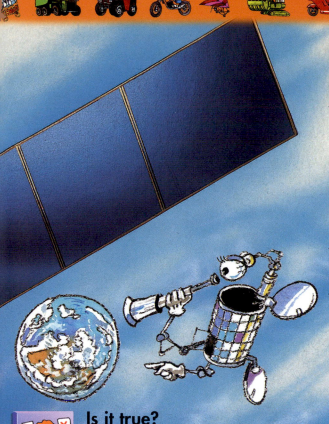

❓ Do satellites ever fall out of the sky?

Yes, accidents can happen! Satellites have crashed into the ocean, and pieces of the empty space station Skylab, were found on farm land in Australia, after it fell back to Earth in 1979.

Satellite crashing into the ocean

Is it true?
There are spy satellites in the sky.

Yes. A big reason for the space race between Russia and America was to spy on each other. Spy satellites use telescopic cameras. Early spy satellites used to drop films to Earth by parachute. Now they take digital photos and beam them home, using secret codes.

21

 Amazing! There are 150,000 bits of space garbage! They fly at incredible speeds, making them very dangerous. A window on a space shuttle was chipped once by a collision with a flake of paint! The American air force keeps track of the largest 8,500 objects in orbit. Letting rubbish drop and burn-up in the atmosphere helps to clean up space.

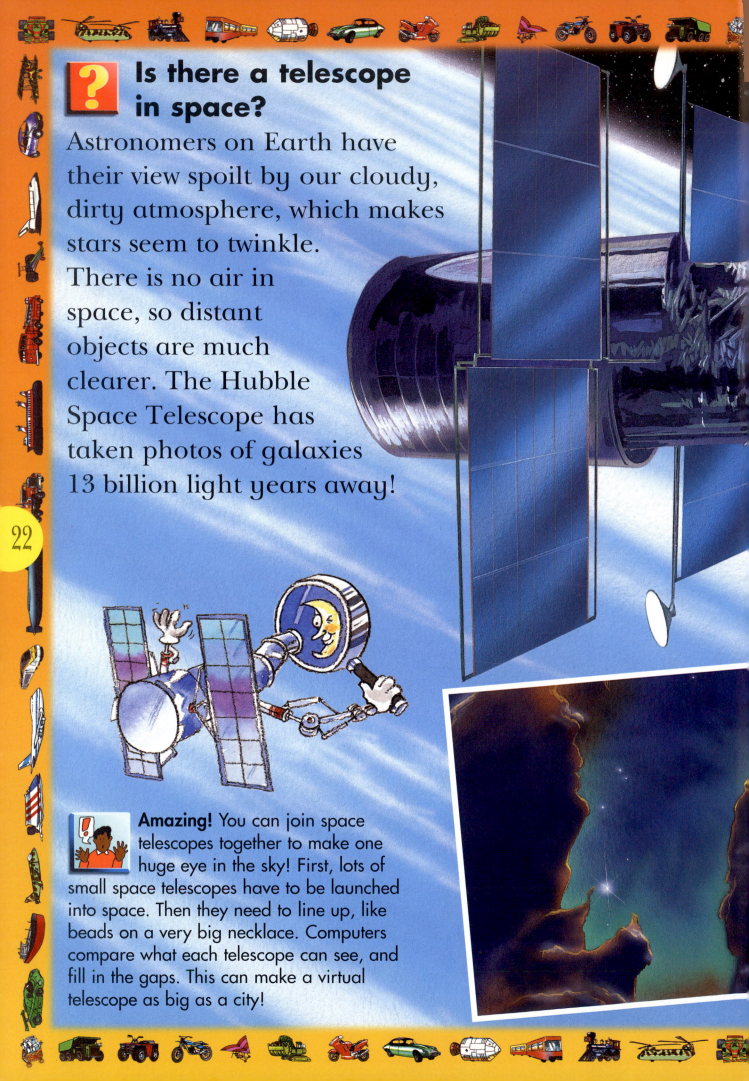

? Is there a telescope in space?

Astronomers on Earth have their view spoilt by our cloudy, dirty atmosphere, which makes stars seem to twinkle. There is no air in space, so distant objects are much clearer. The Hubble Space Telescope has taken photos of galaxies 13 billion light years away!

Amazing! You can join space telescopes together to make one huge eye in the sky! First, lots of small space telescopes have to be launched into space. Then they need to line up, like beads on a very big necklace. Computers compare what each telescope can see, and fill in the gaps. This can make a virtual telescope as big as a city!

Repairing Hubble

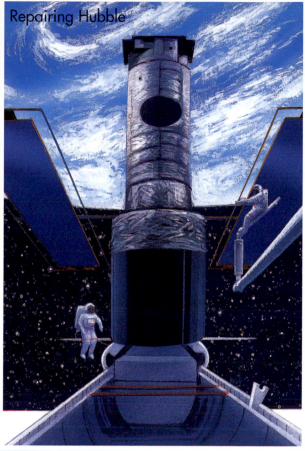

Hubble telescope

Is it true?
The Hubble telescope can see stars being born.

Yes. The Hubble image here shows stars being made in the Eagle Nebula. The fingers of cloud are bigger than our entire solar system. They are made of gas and dust, which slowly collects into lumps. As they grow, the lumps become hotter, creating thousands of new stars!

Eagle Nebula

What happens if the telescope breaks down?

Hubble had to be fixed by astronauts almost as soon as it was launched. The mirror it uses to collect images was the wrong shape, making pictures fuzzy. In December 1993 a shuttle met up with Hubble, and astronauts adjusted the mirror successfully.

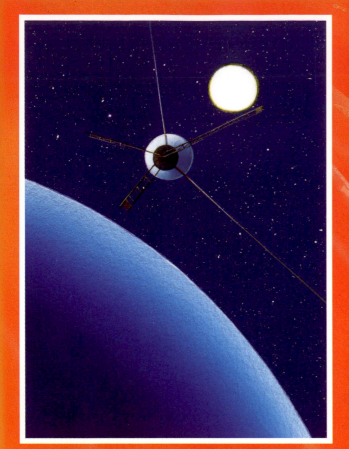

Voyager probe passing Neptune

24

? Which voyagers visited all the planets?

Humans can't travel to other planets yet. A trip to Mars would need much bigger spacecraft than the shuttle. Instead, unmanned space probes like Voyager can travel through the solar system, sending home pictures of the planets.

 Is it true?
A Mariner took photos of Mercury.

Yes. A very successful space probe called Mariner 10 visited the planet Mercury three times in the 1970s. As well as taking photos, Mariner discovered Mercury's strange magnetic field, and signs of ice at the poles.

? Which probe got too hot?

Four Venera probes have landed on Venus. The temperature there is a sweaty 1020°. As if that wasn't nasty enough, the clouds rain pure sulphuric acid!

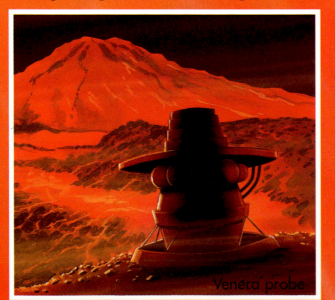

Venera probe

Cassini probe

Amazing!
The Huygens probe will parachute on to Saturn's largest moon in 2004. Huygens is hitching there on a Saturn probe, Cassini. Titan is bigger than the planets Mercury or Pluto. Titan has its own, cloudy atmosphere, blocking our view of its surface. Titan might be covered in an ocean, so Huygens is designed to float!

? Which probe visited a comet?

Giotto was made to visit Halley's Comet as it passed Earth in 1986. Giotto had a special shield to protect it from the dust of the comet's tail. The probe took measurements and photographs from 370 miles away, revealing the rocky heart of the comet.

Giotto passing Halley's Comet

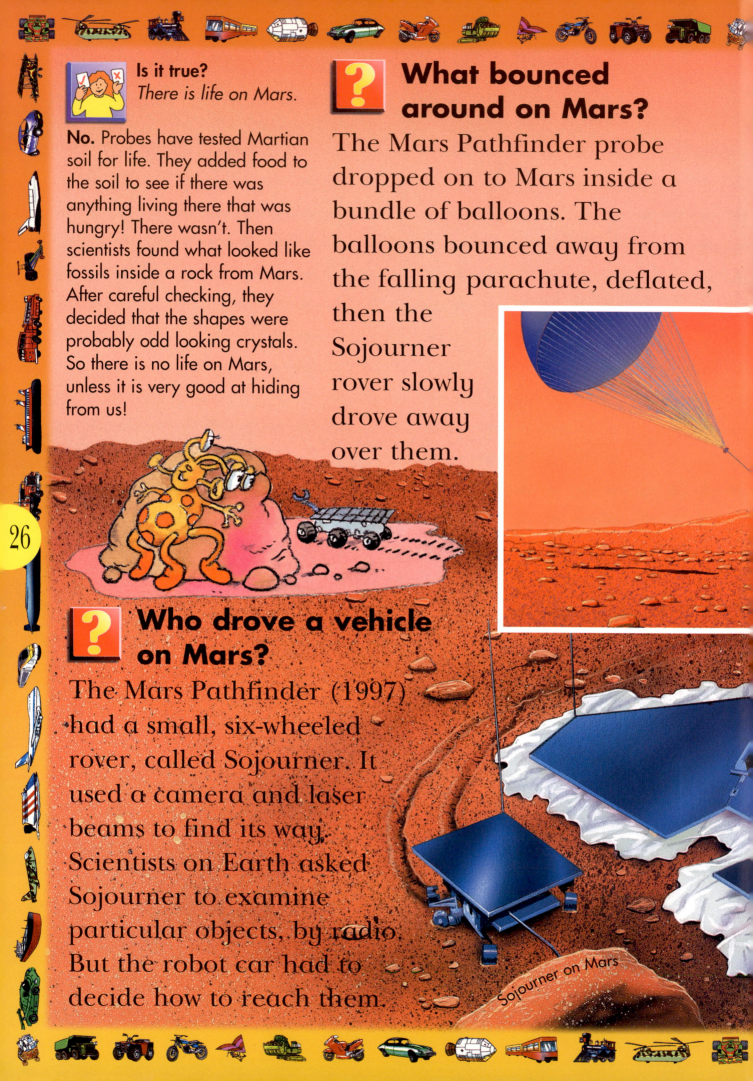

Is it true?
There is life on Mars.

No. Probes have tested Martian soil for life. They added food to the soil to see if there was anything living there that was hungry! There wasn't. Then scientists found what looked like fossils inside a rock from Mars. After careful checking, they decided that the shapes were probably odd looking crystals. So there is no life on Mars, unless it is very good at hiding from us!

What bounced around on Mars?

The Mars Pathfinder probe dropped on to Mars inside a bundle of balloons. The balloons bounced away from the falling parachute, deflated, then the Sojourner rover slowly drove away over them.

Who drove a vehicle on Mars?

The Mars Pathfinder (1997) had a small, six-wheeled rover, called Sojourner. It used a camera and laser beams to find its way. Scientists on Earth asked Sojourner to examine particular objects, by radio. But the robot car had to decide how to reach them.

Sojourner on Mars

❓ Did Vikings really land on Mars?

Two space probes, called Viking 1 and Viking 2, landed on Mars in the 1970s. They took 3,000 photos, some in 3-D, and beamed them back to Earth. The Viking probes also measured weather patterns and examined the soil for signs of life. They didn't find any aliens.

Mars Pathfinder landing

Mars probe

Amazing! For 20 years before Pathfinder, several probes sent to Mars ended in disaster. 16 probes from Russia either exploded on launch, missed the planet, or crashed into its surface. The American probe Observer exploded as it entered Mars's orbit. Some probes just went missing. Nobody knows why.

Who is building a new space station?

America is leading a group of countries to build an international space station (ISS). The space shuttle is used to deliver parts. Most are made in America, but there are Japanese, Russian, Canadian and European parts as well. ISS uses giant solar panels to make its own electricity.

John Glenn

Amazing! John Glenn went to space at the age of 77. Sensors on his skin were used to monitor his health. His record-breaking flight happened 36 years after his first space trip, when he was the first American to orbit the Earth.

International space station

❓ Will there ever be a Moon Base?

If space gets a lot busier it will make sense to use the Moon as a base. The Moon's low gravity lets big spacecraft take off and land easily compared to Earth.

Future Moon base

Is it true?
People can be "buried" in space.

Yes. A cheap new rocket called Pegasus has made space funerals possible. The rocket delivered 25 people's ashes into space in 1997. For under $5,000 each, the ashes were scattered in orbit. They will drift back to Earth after a few years.

❓ Will I ever go to space?

Only a few people become astronauts. But tourists may soon be able to vacation in space. There are plans to use empty shuttle fuel tanks as the rooms of a space hotel!

Space hotel of the future

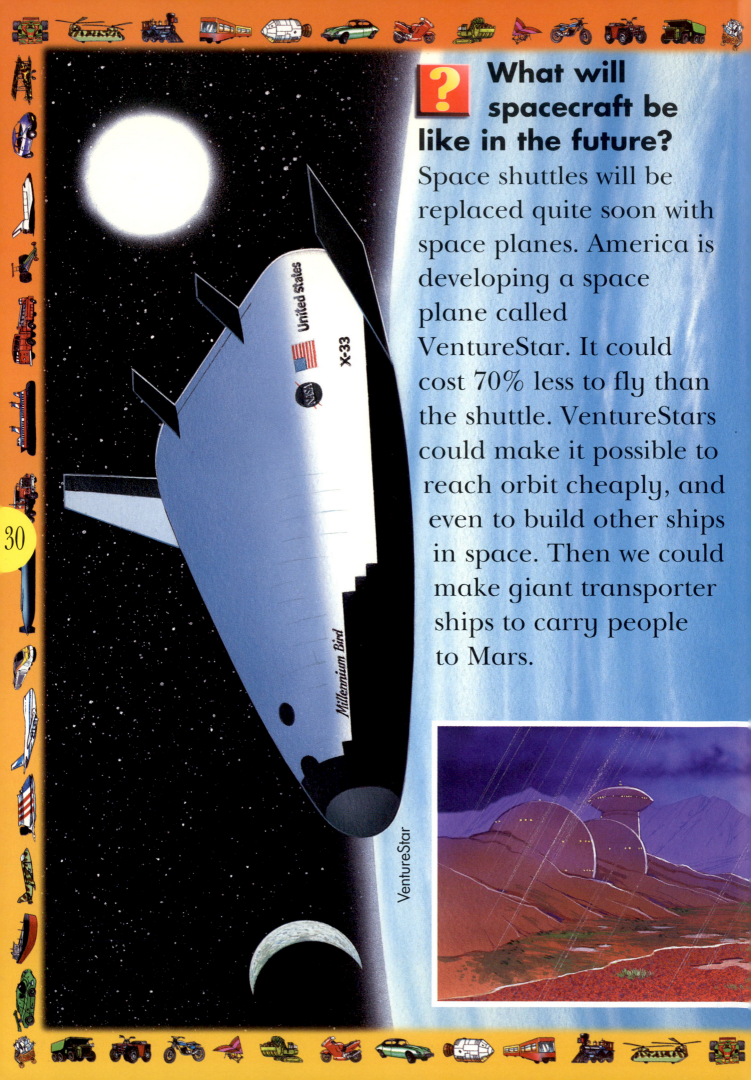

? What will spacecraft be like in the future?

Space shuttles will be replaced quite soon with space planes. America is developing a space plane called VentureStar. It could cost 70% less to fly than the shuttle. VentureStars could make it possible to reach orbit cheaply, and even to build other ships in space. Then we could make giant transporter ships to carry people to Mars.

United States

X-33

Millennium Bird

VentureStar

? Will we ever visit other solar systems?

The nearest star to our Sun is 4.3 light years away. The shuttle would take 158,000 years to get there! We will need amazing new spacecraft before we visit other solar systems.

Amazing! You might travel to space on a laser beam! Scientists in America are testing a laser that heats a pocket of air under a spacecraft. The very hot air pushes the craft upwards. No energy is wasted lifting heavy fuel off the ground.

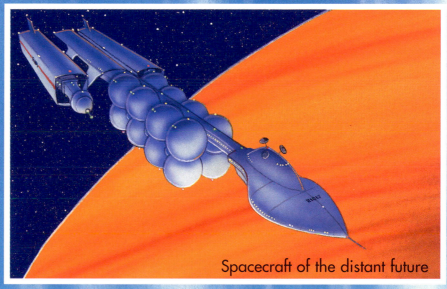

Spacecraft of the distant future

? Will we colonize Mars?

Robots might be able to build a Mars base. Humans would have to wear space suits outside, but would live in airtight habitats, with plants and animals. Genetically modified plants could grow, which would create breathable air and water, making the whole planet habitable.

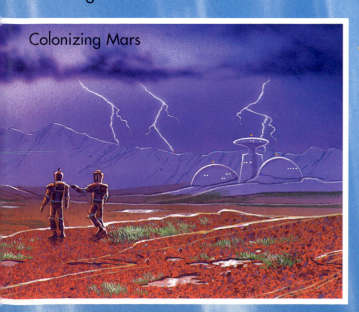

Colonizing Mars